ISBN-13; 978-1542898300

Printed in The United States Of America

Letter Wonders

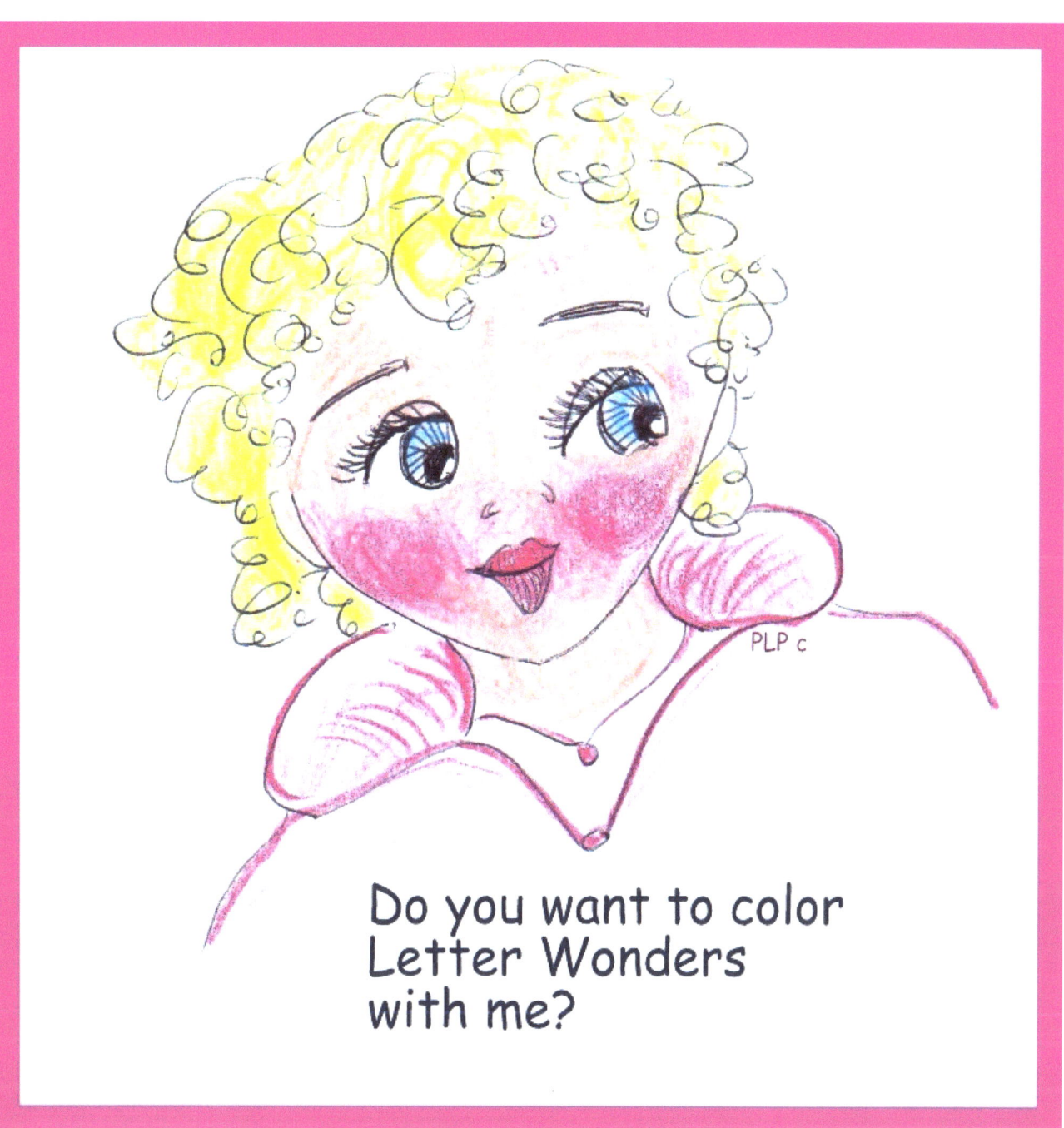

Do you want to color
Letter Wonders
with me?

Welcome to a coloring adventure with Awesome Letter A!

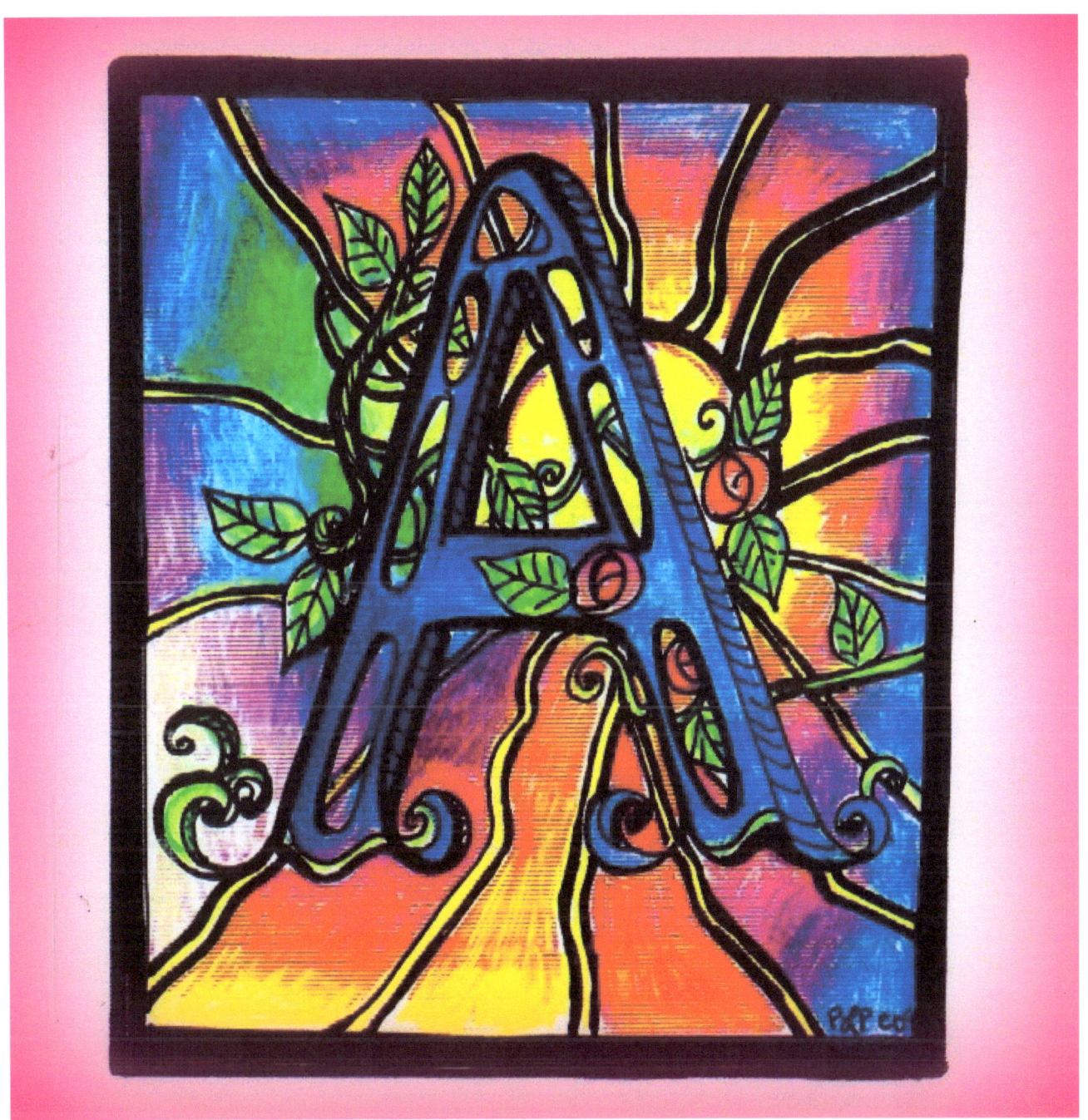

The Awesome Letter A
Coloring Book

By Peggy Louise Parrish
C. 2017

You now are in an adventure with Awesome Letter A. There is no end to how an A can be designed or colored. These are some unique designed As and a few coloring ideas and examples. Use your imagination and your favorite art medium to bring them into your style. This book challenges those of you who enjoy coloring therapy and those just curious enough to this Awesome Letter A Collection.

Perhaps your first name or last name begins with an A letter. You have permission to make a few "in house" copies of the pages that you want to color multiple ways .Maybe you want to make one into a card for someone. Keep the artist initials PLP on the page and feel free to write colored by and your name if you want at the bottom of your work.

The preferred medium for this work is usually quality colored pencils. If you want to try watercolor pencils, markers or paints be sure you put a scrap piece of paper behind your work while you are doing it to avoid color bleeding through onto the next page. Now...enjoy....

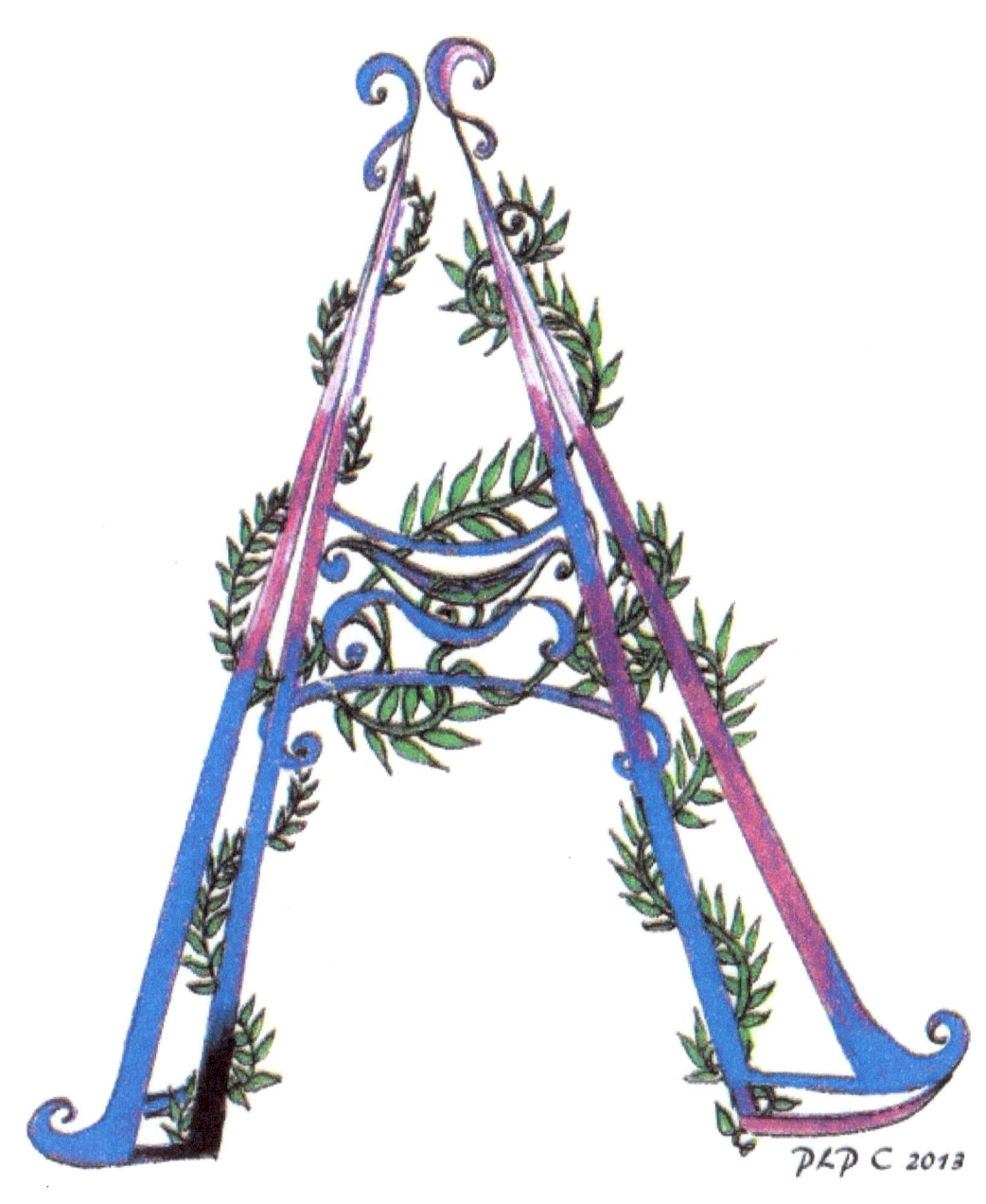

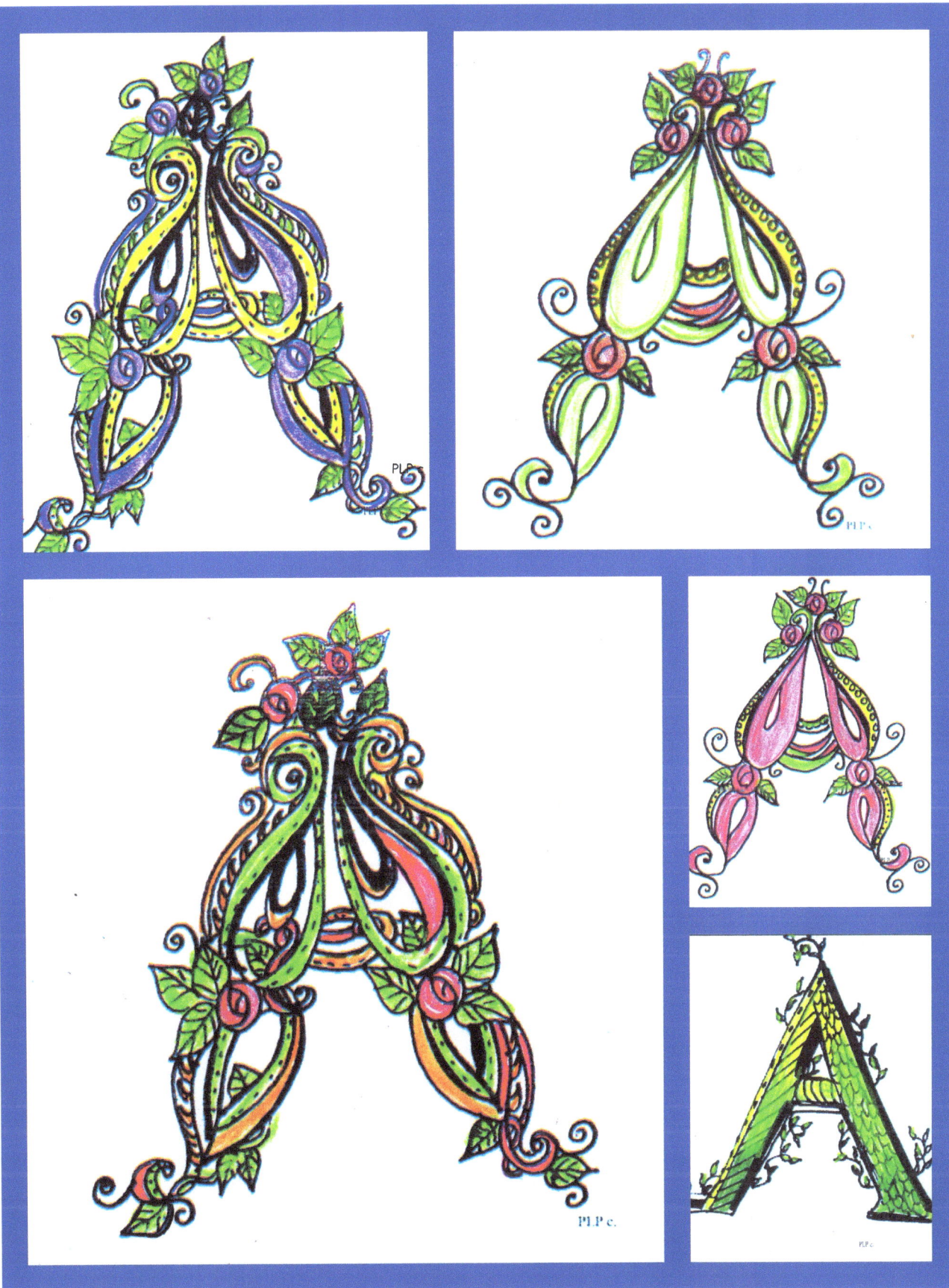

11

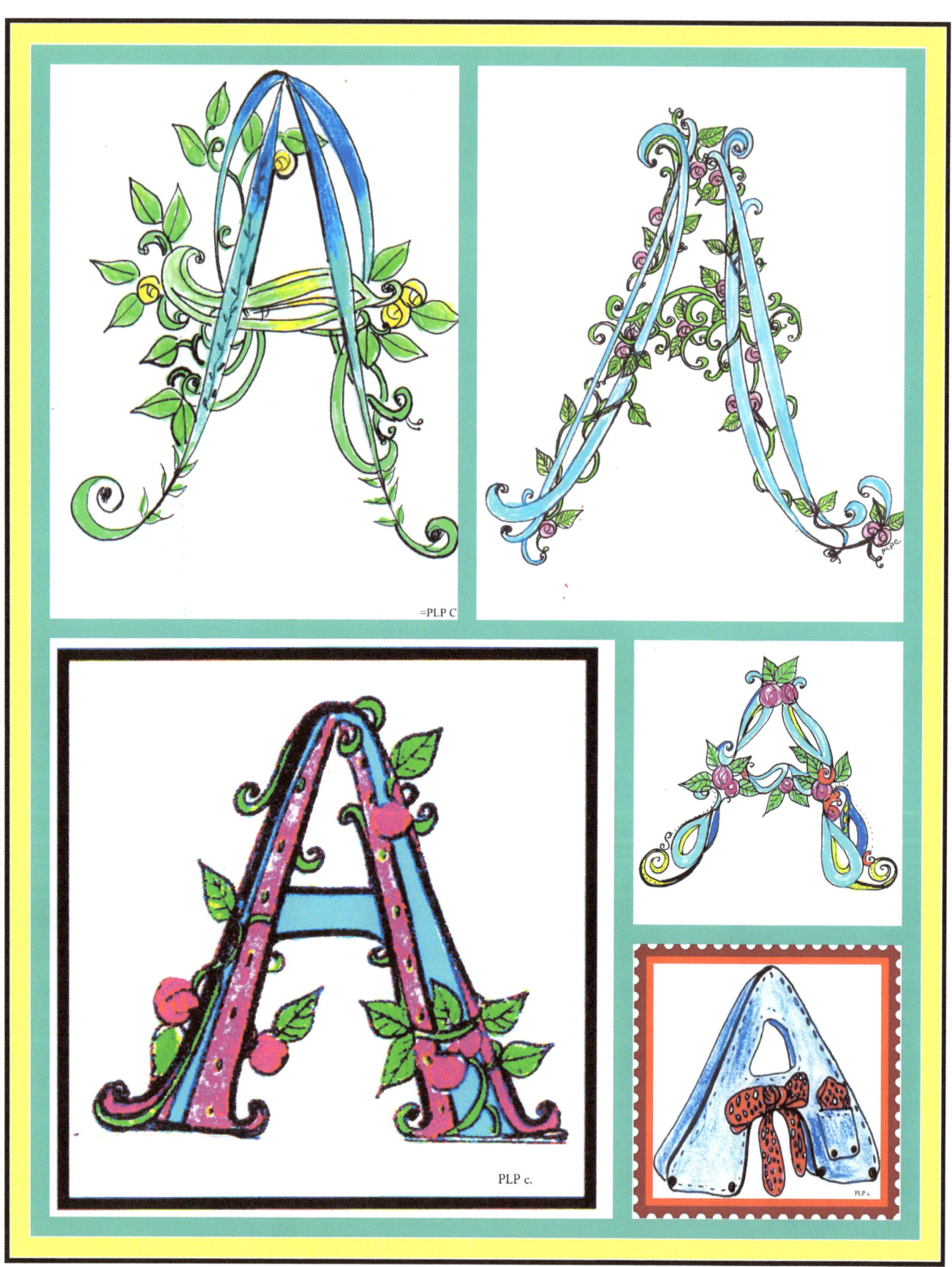

=PLP C

PLP c.

PLP c.

Awesome

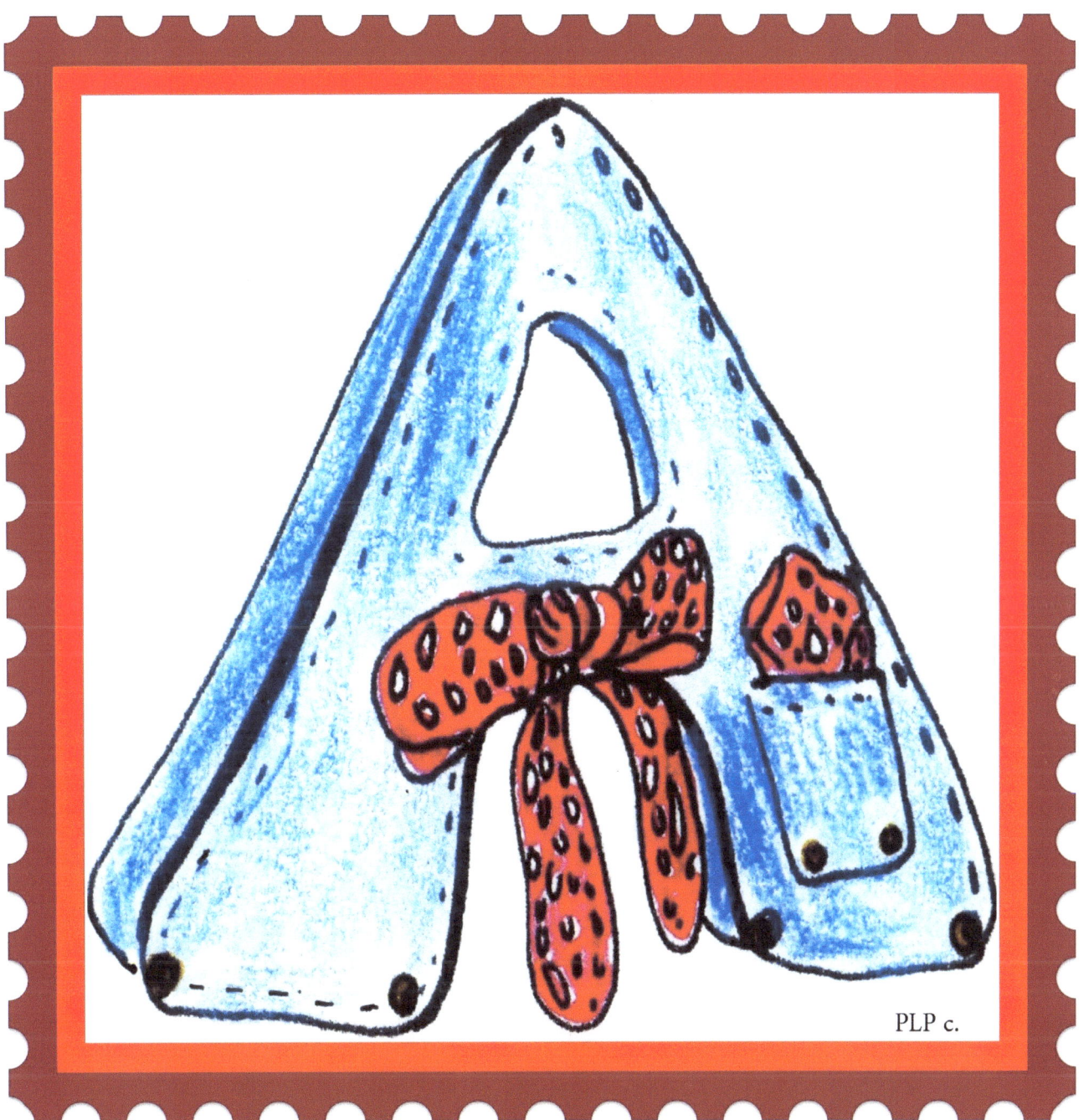

PLP c.

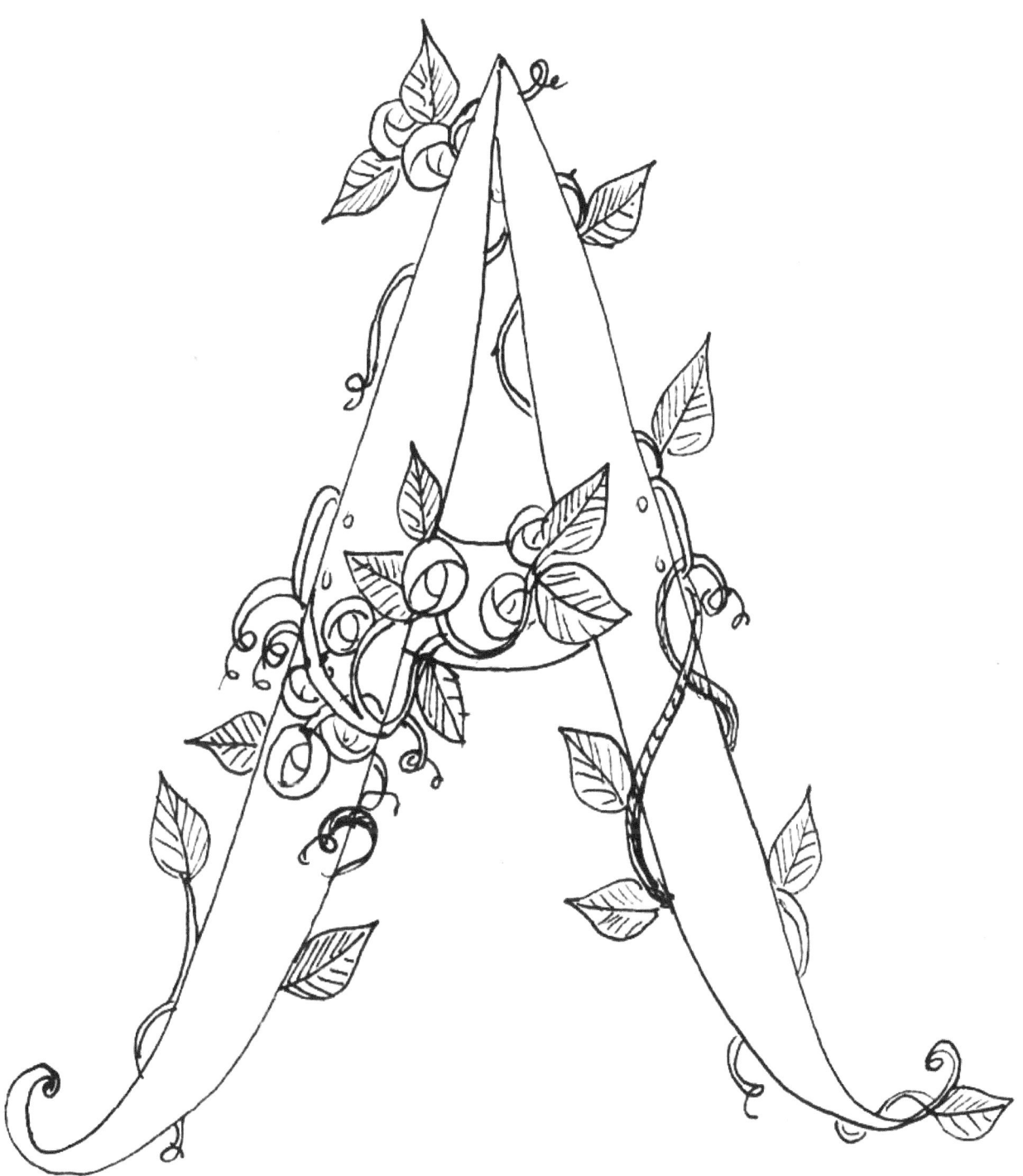

PLP c.

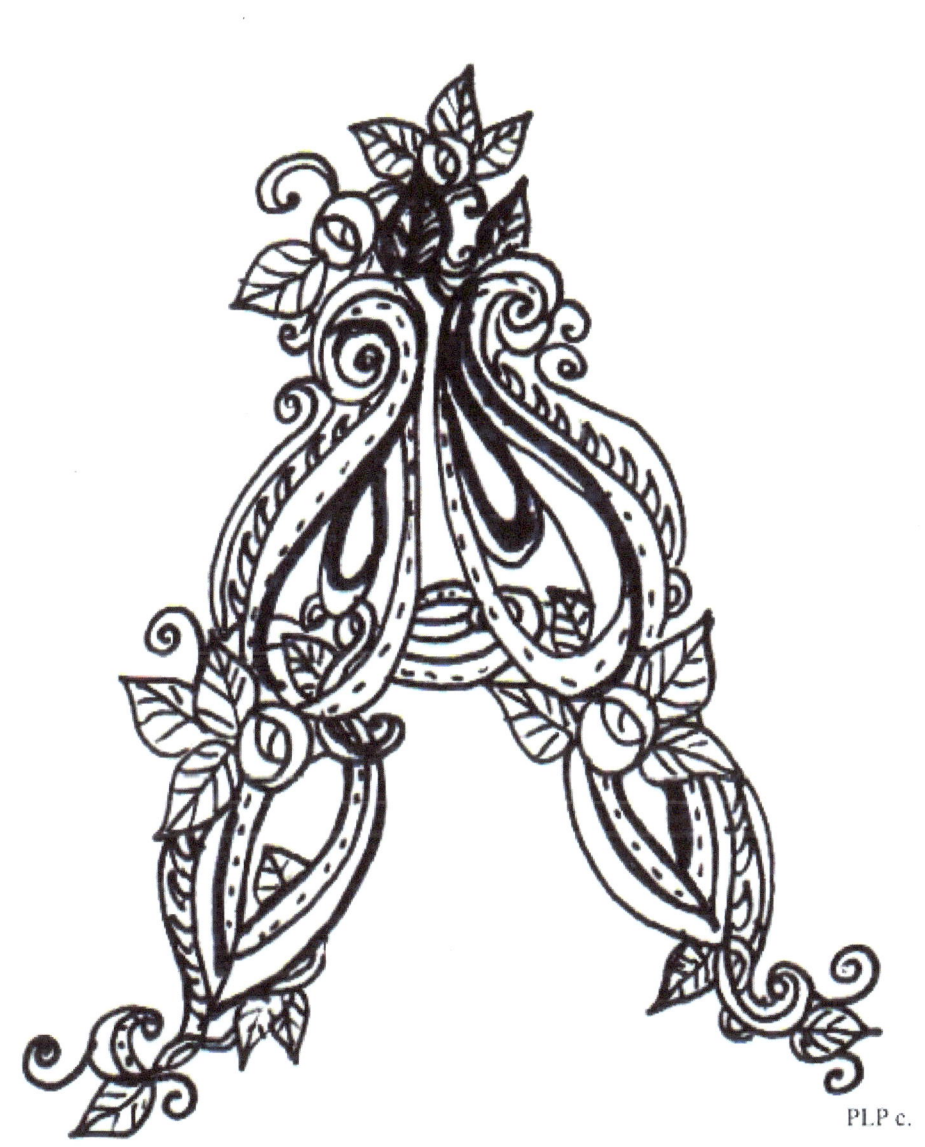

PLP c.

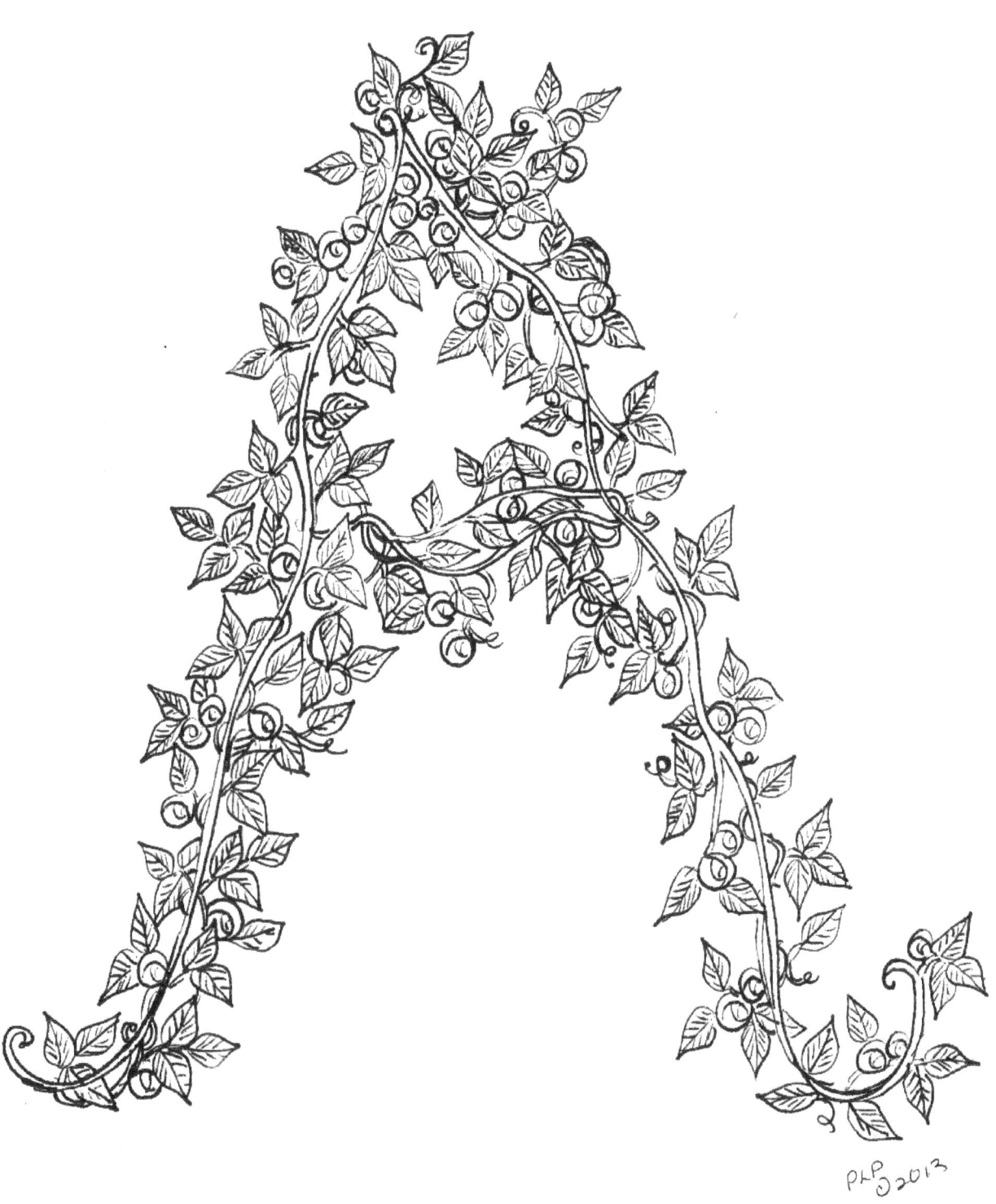

PLP c.

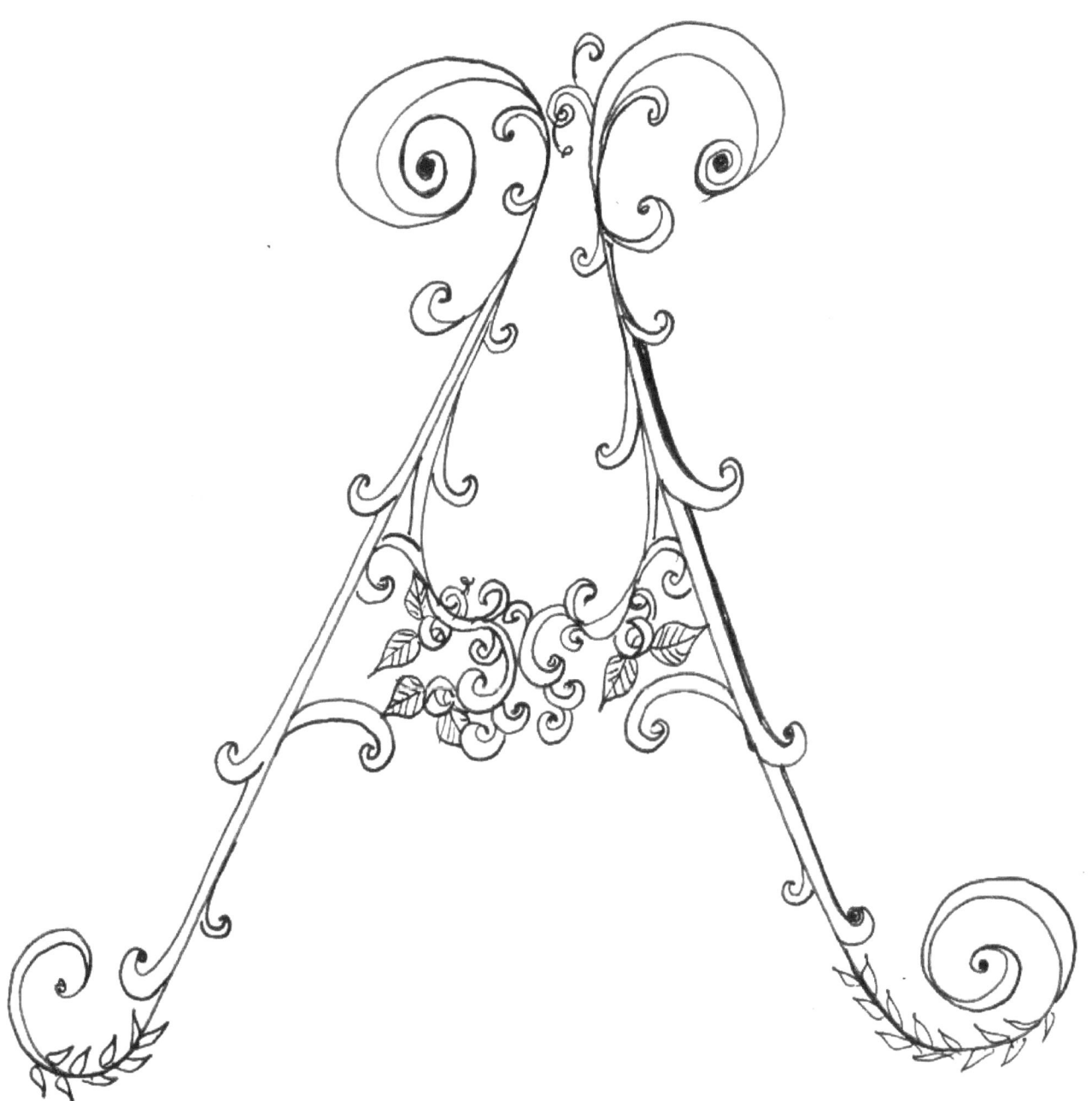

PLP c.

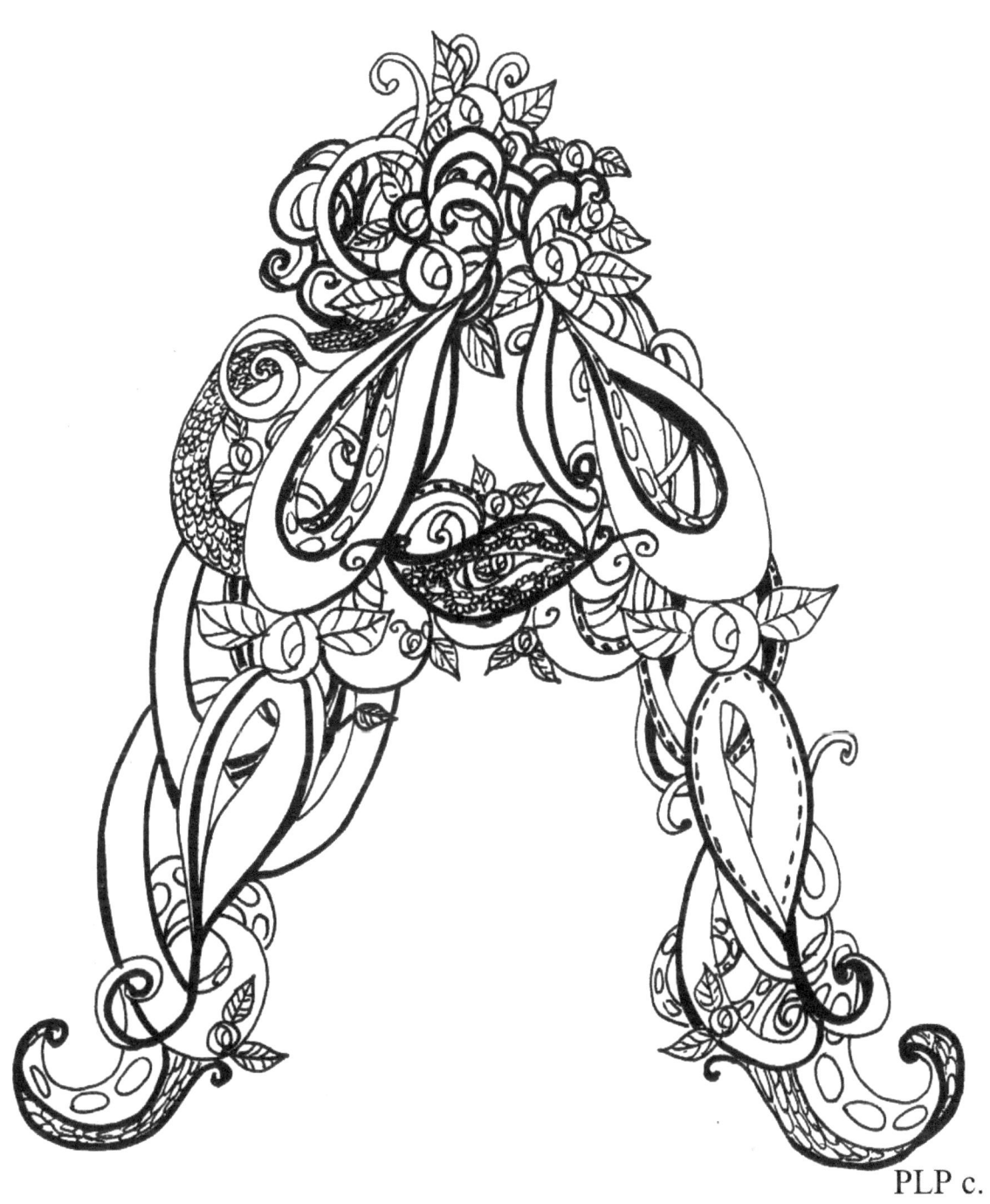

PLP c.

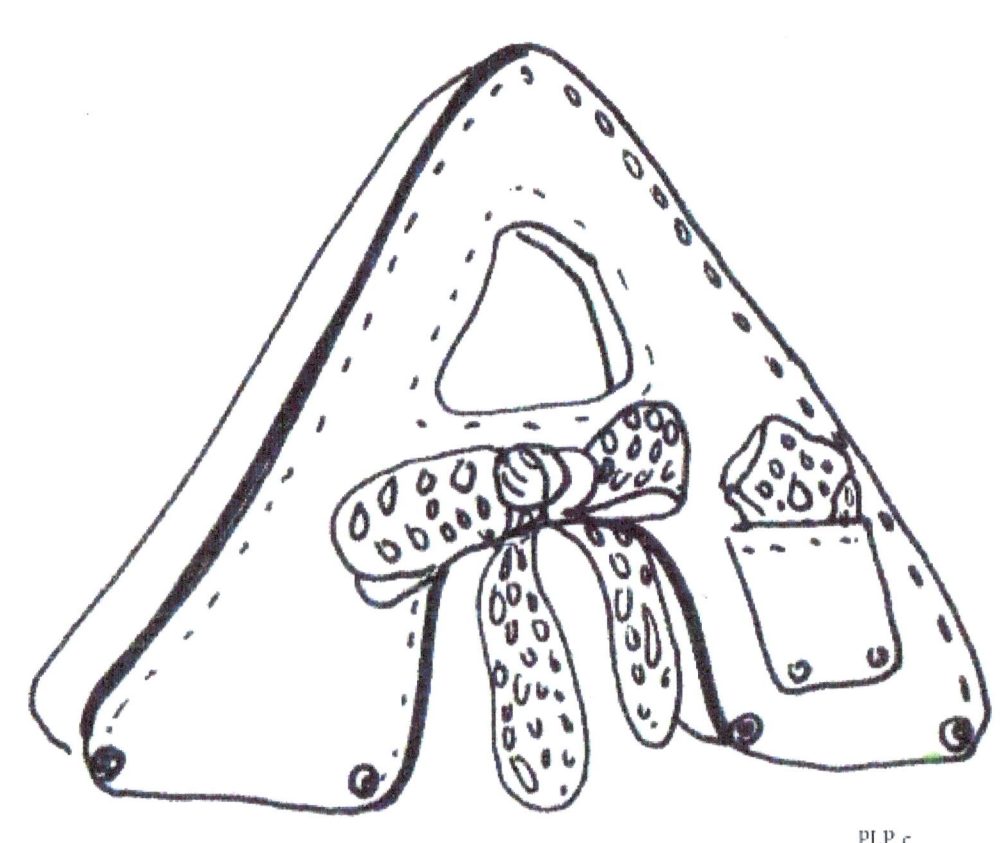

PLP c.

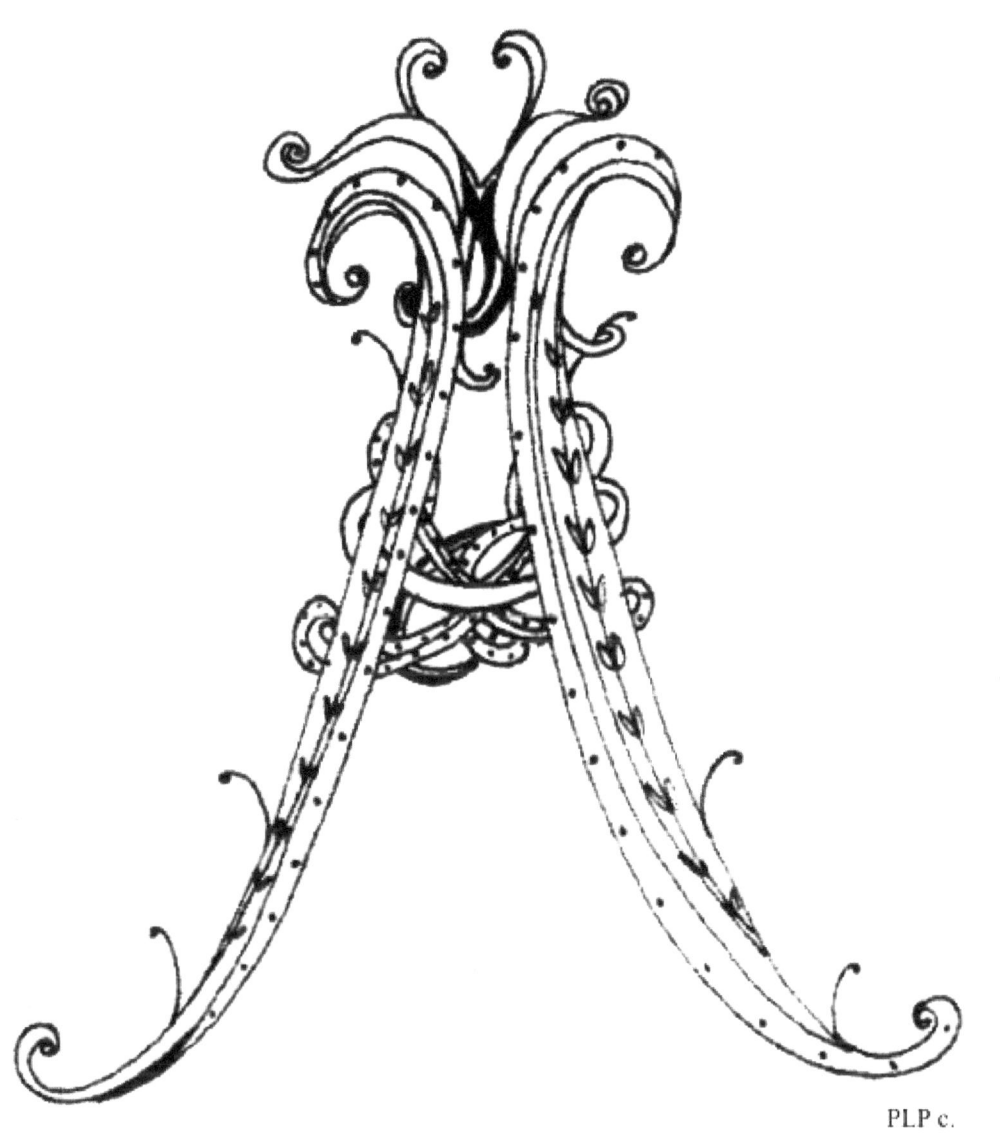

PLP c.

PLP c.

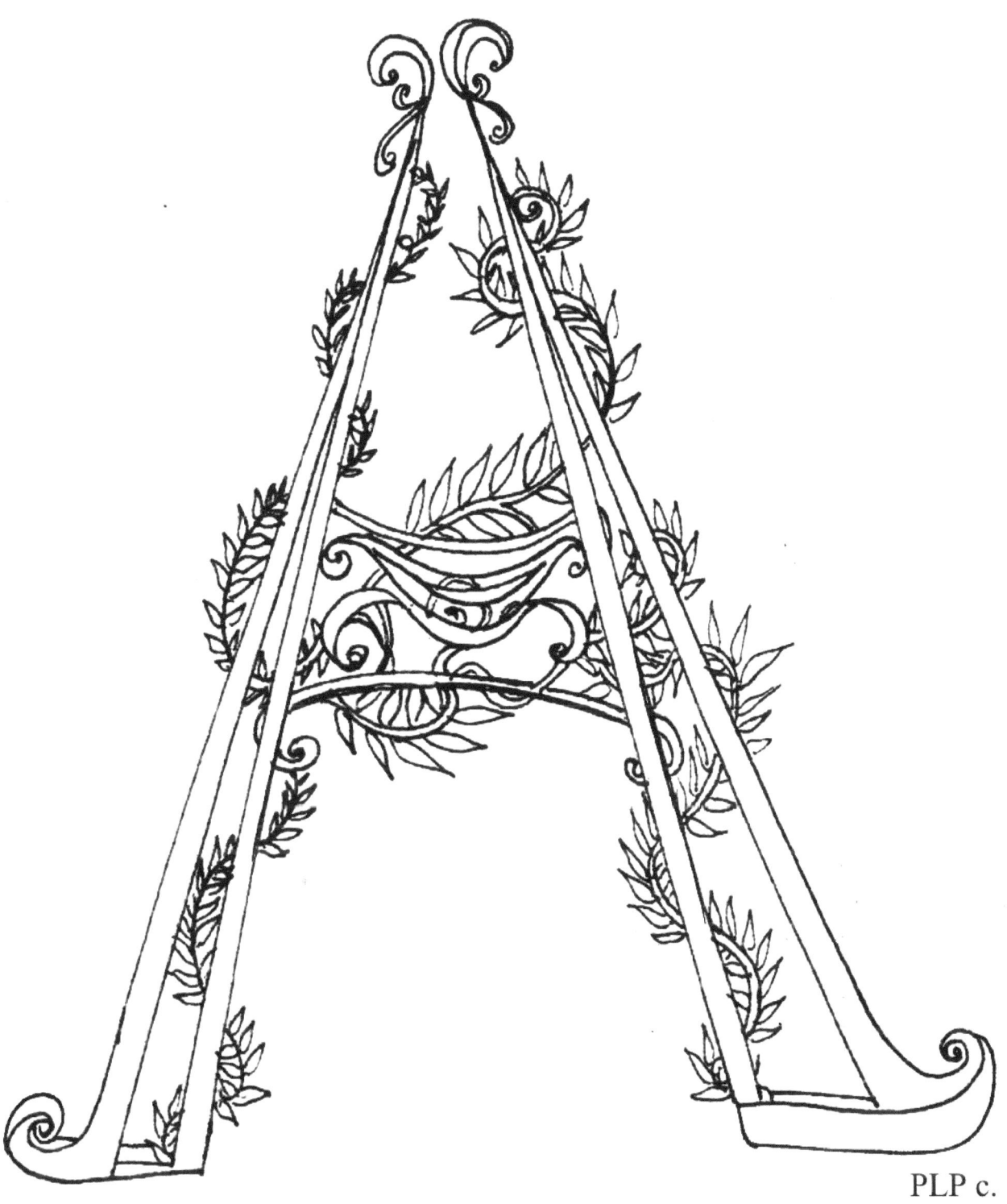

PLP c.

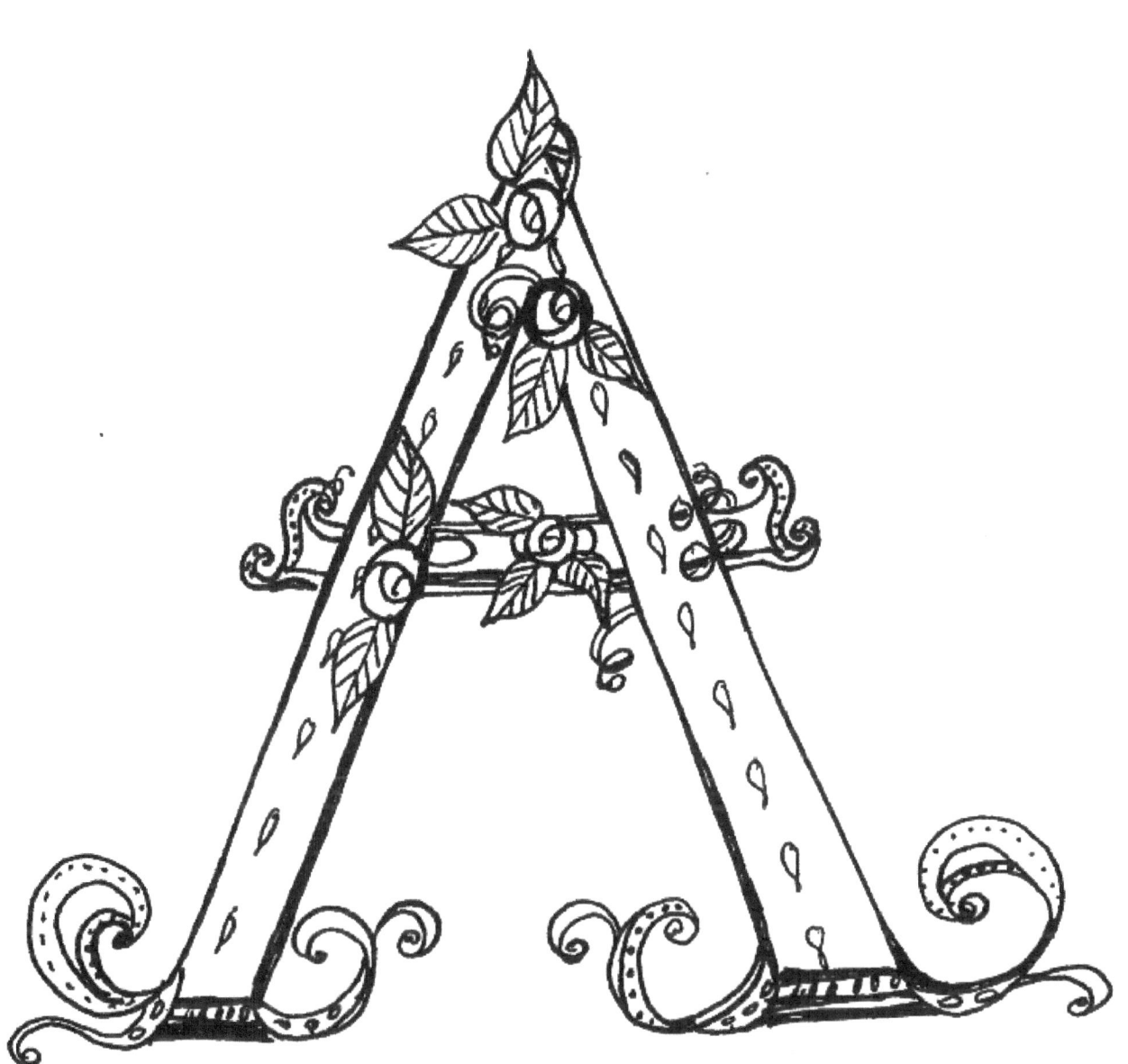

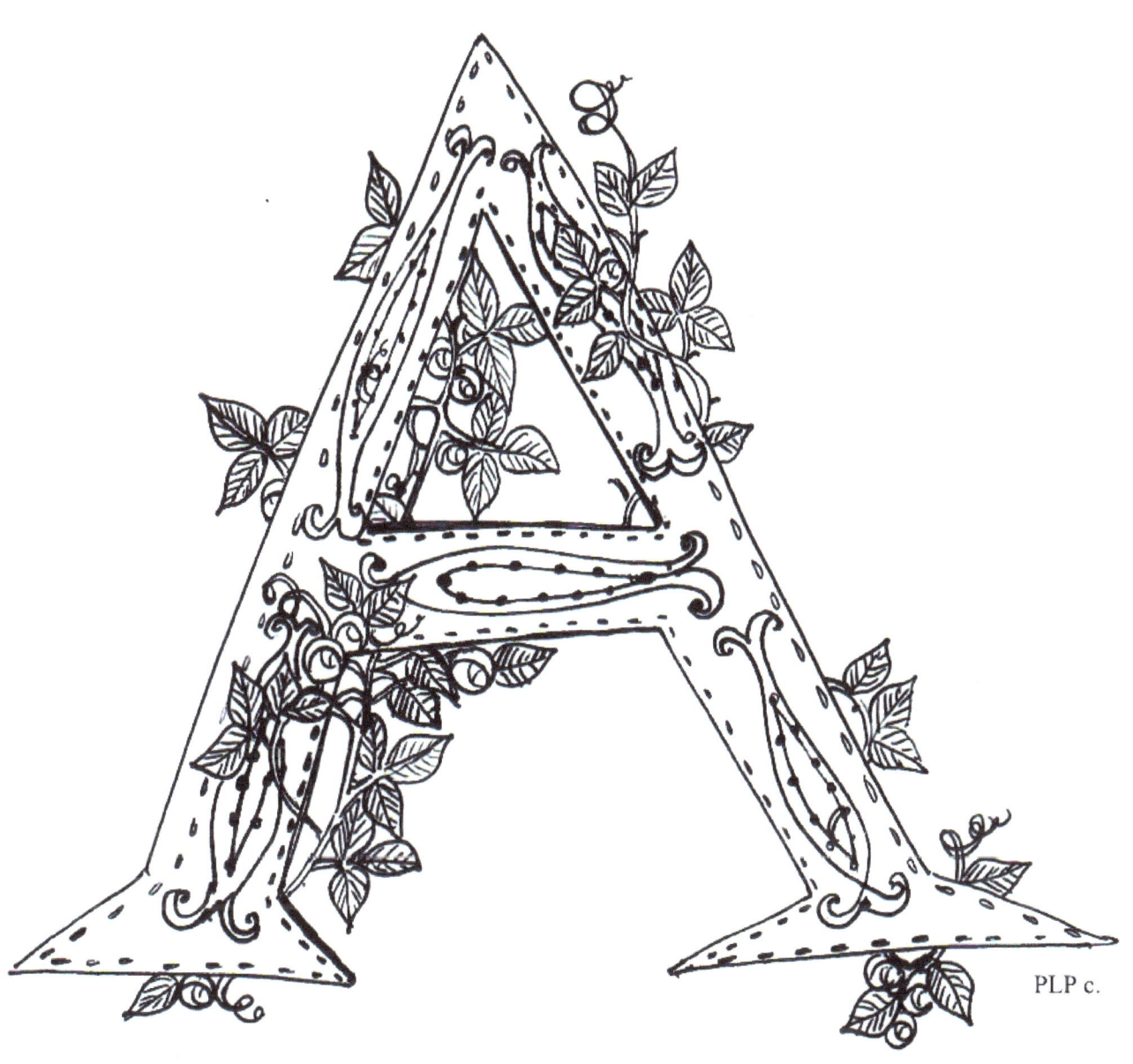

PLP c.

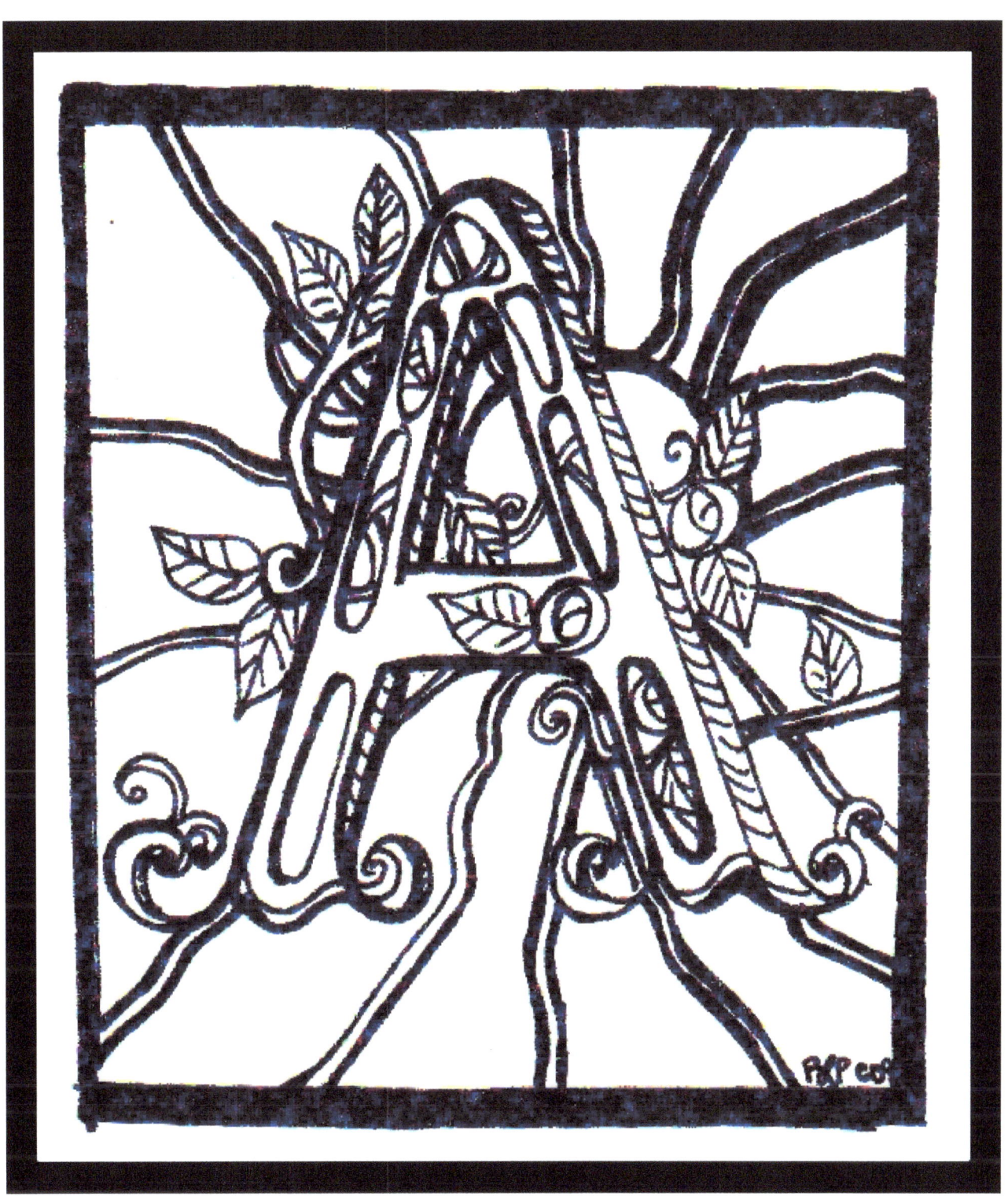

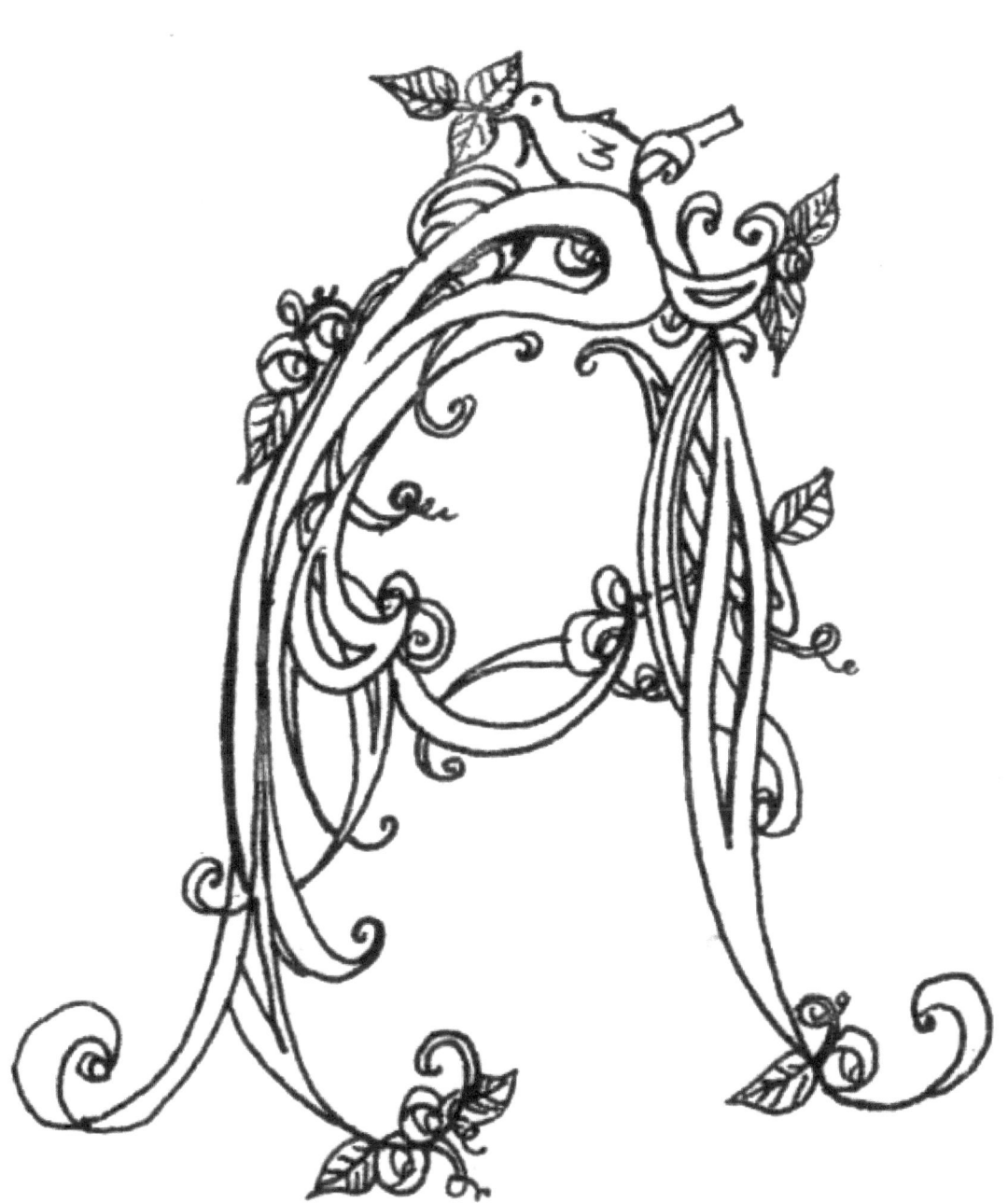

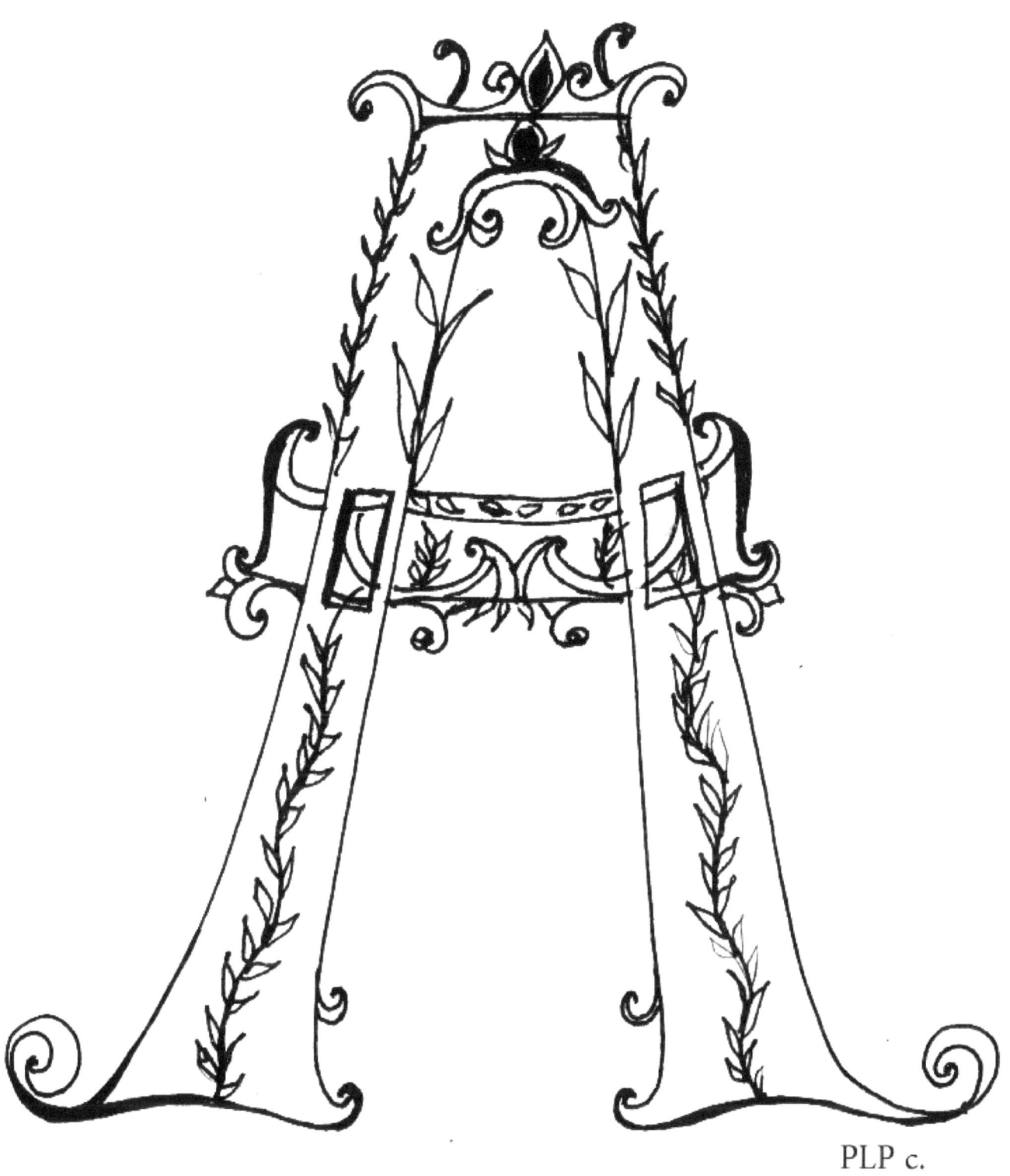

PLP c.

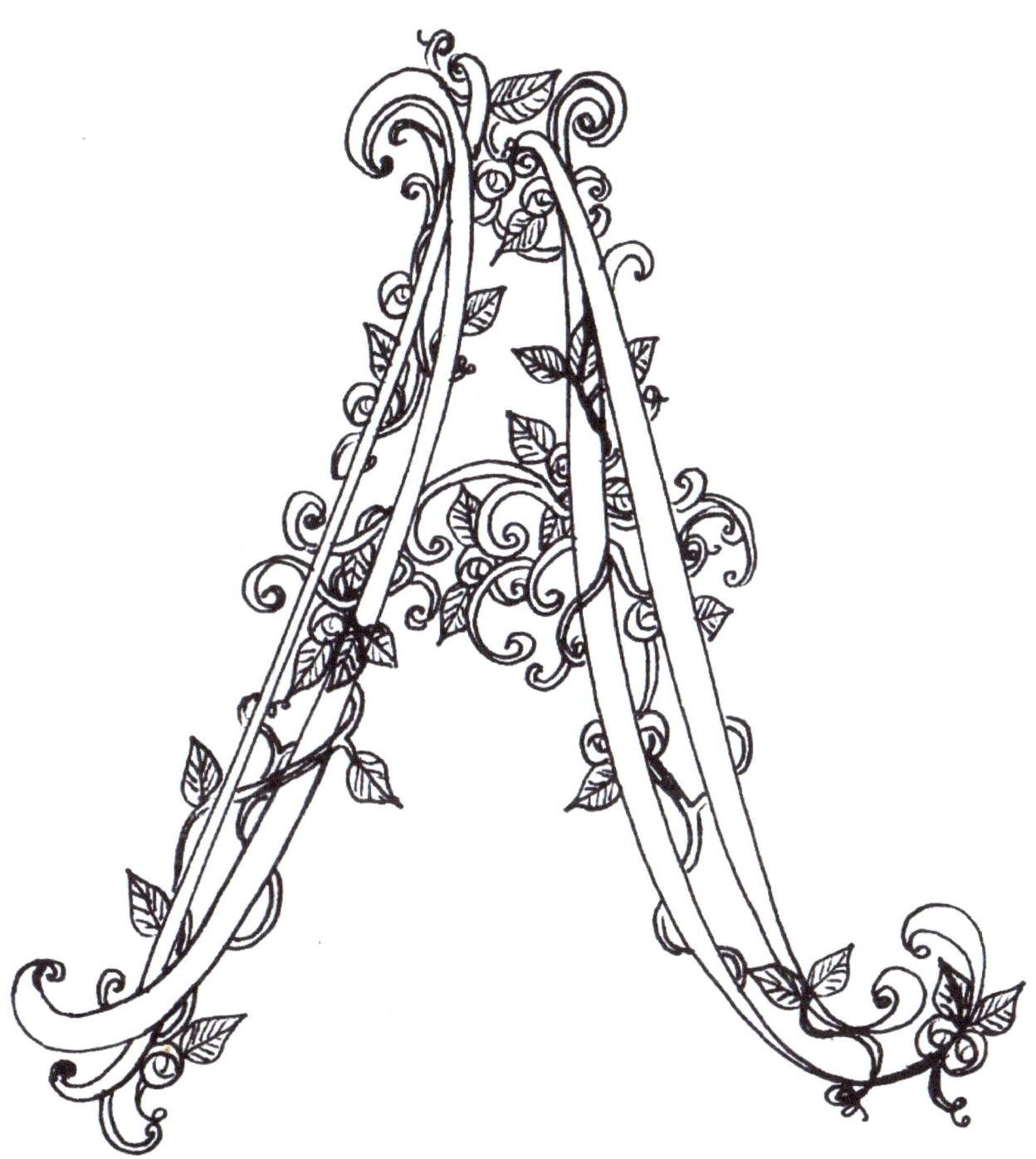

PLP c.

Try these beautiful A names

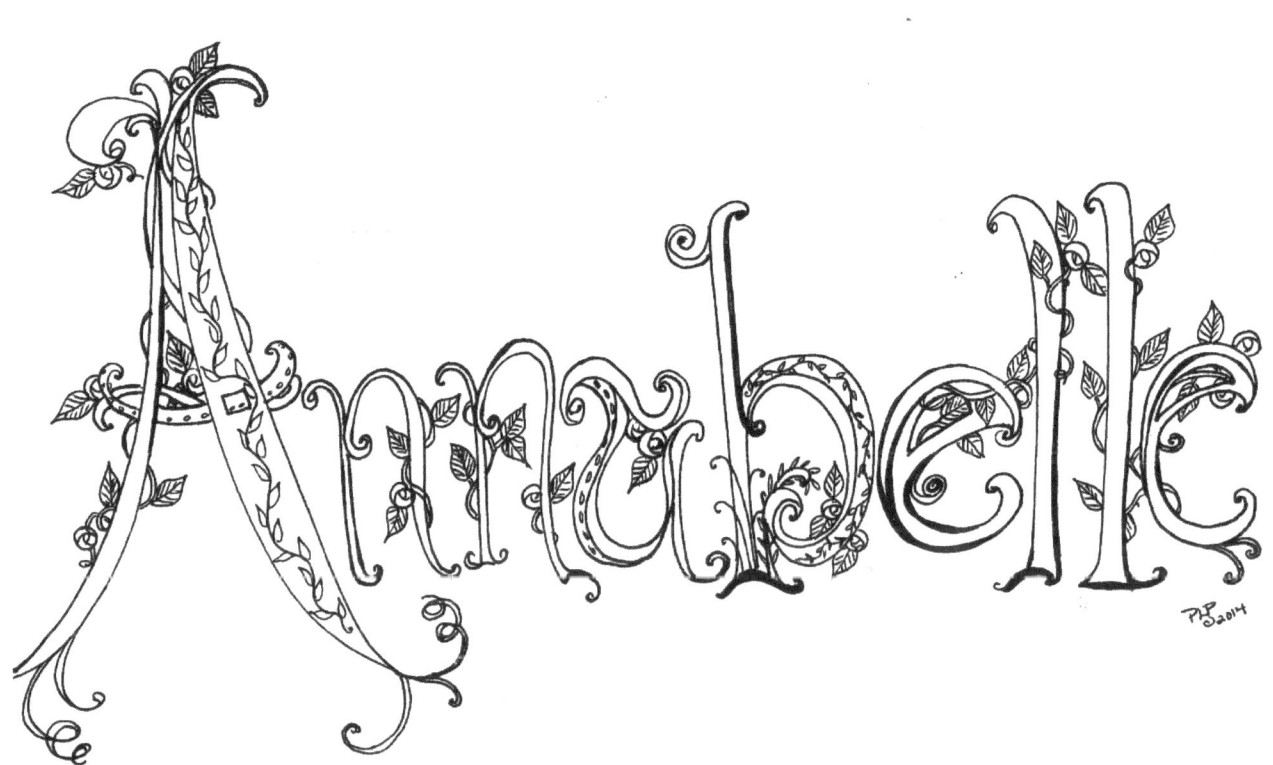

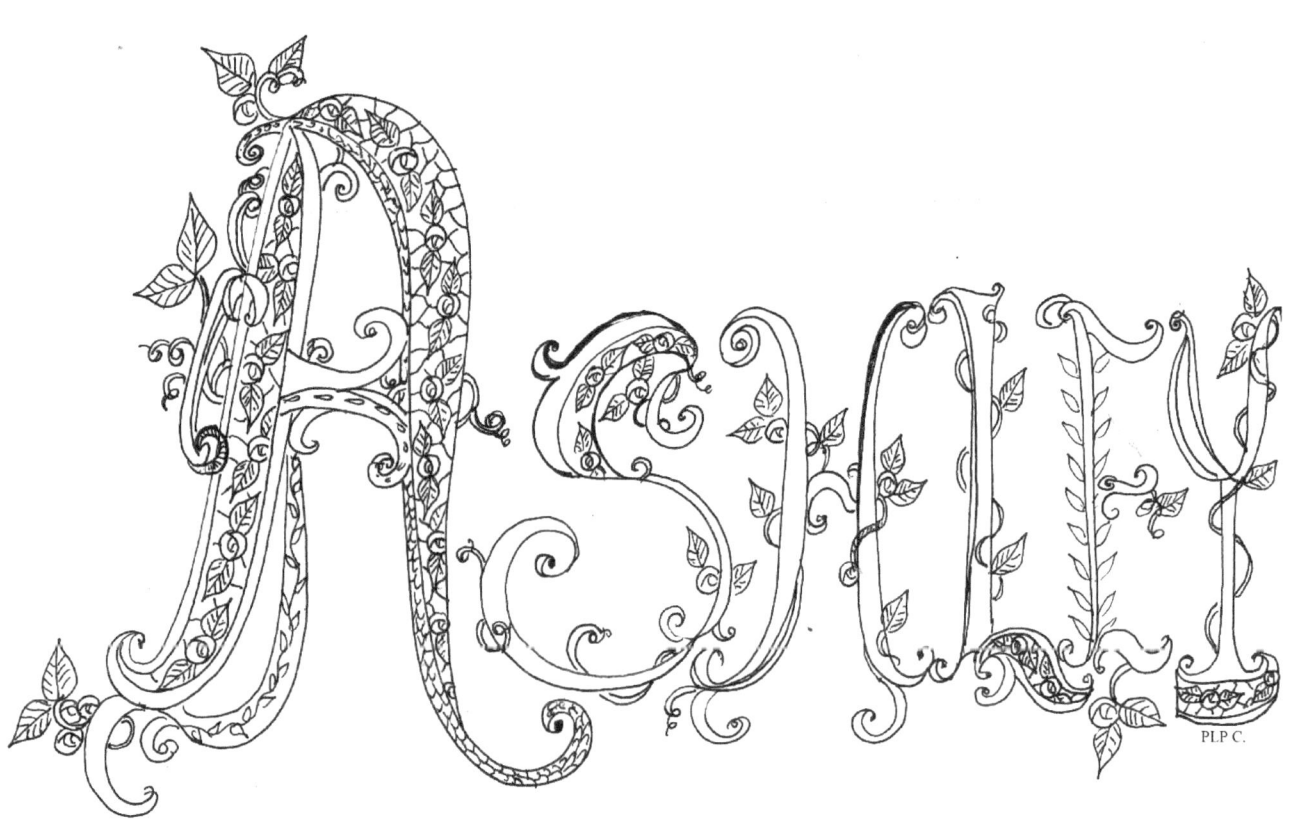

PLP C.

51

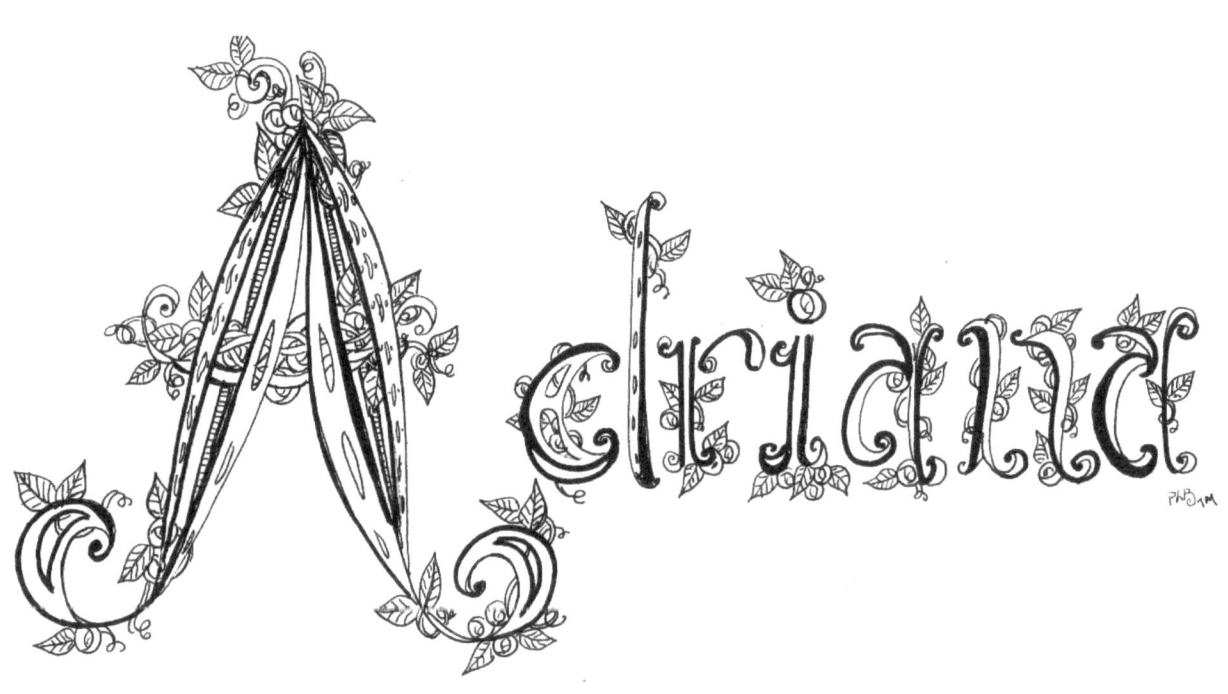

Did you find this letter in the coloring pages?

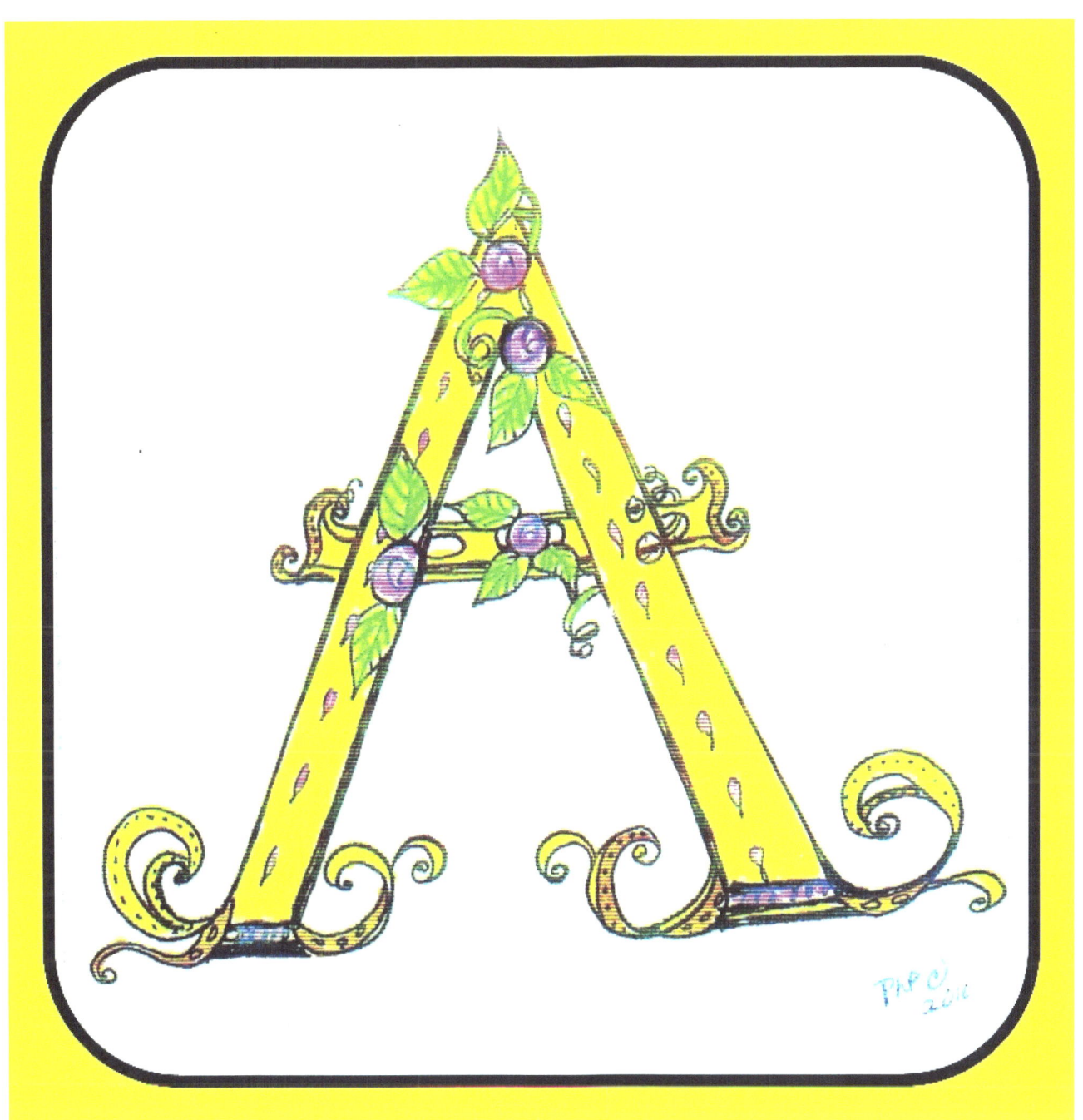

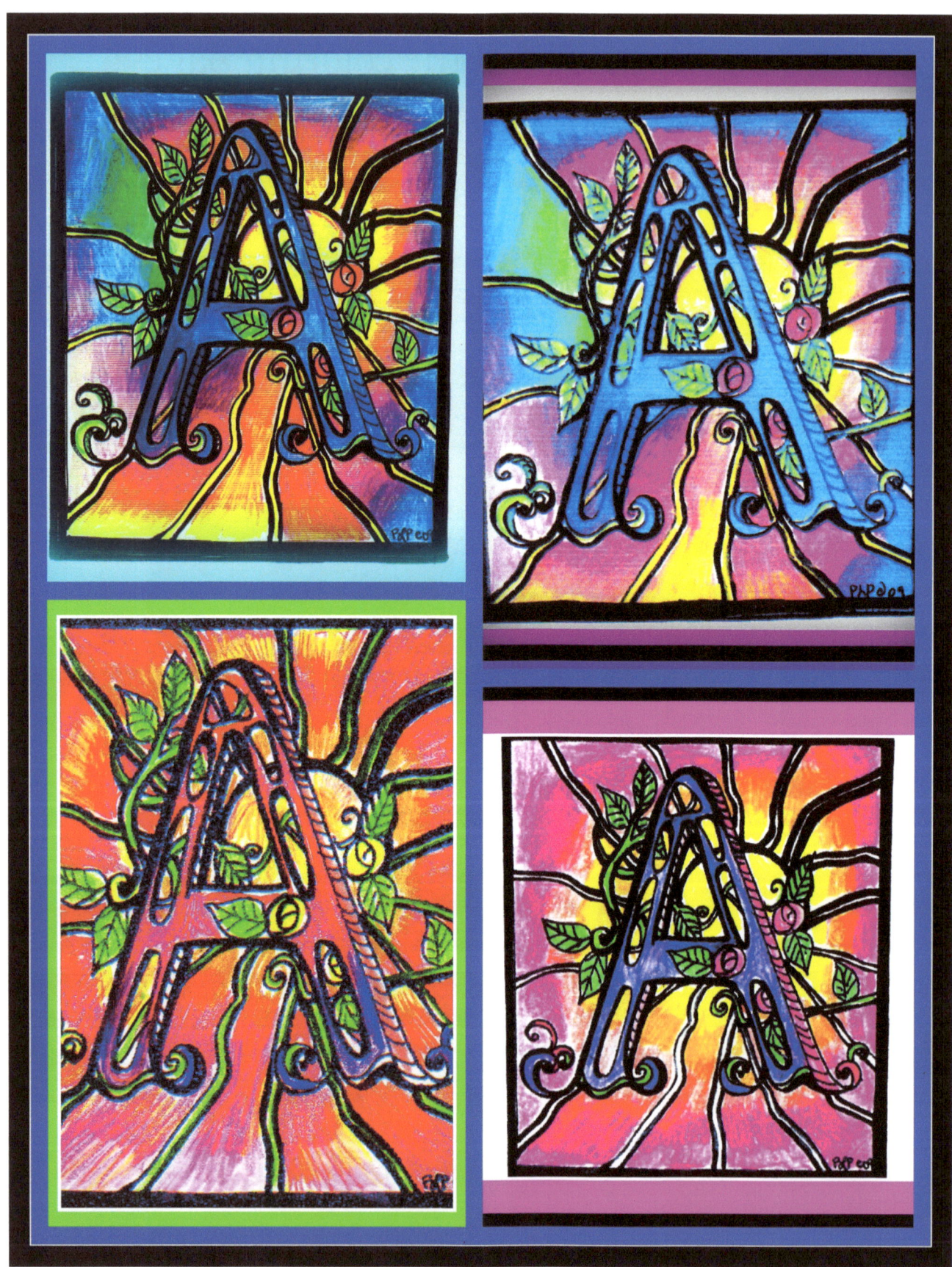

If you enjoyed the A letters in this book check out

the other letter books by

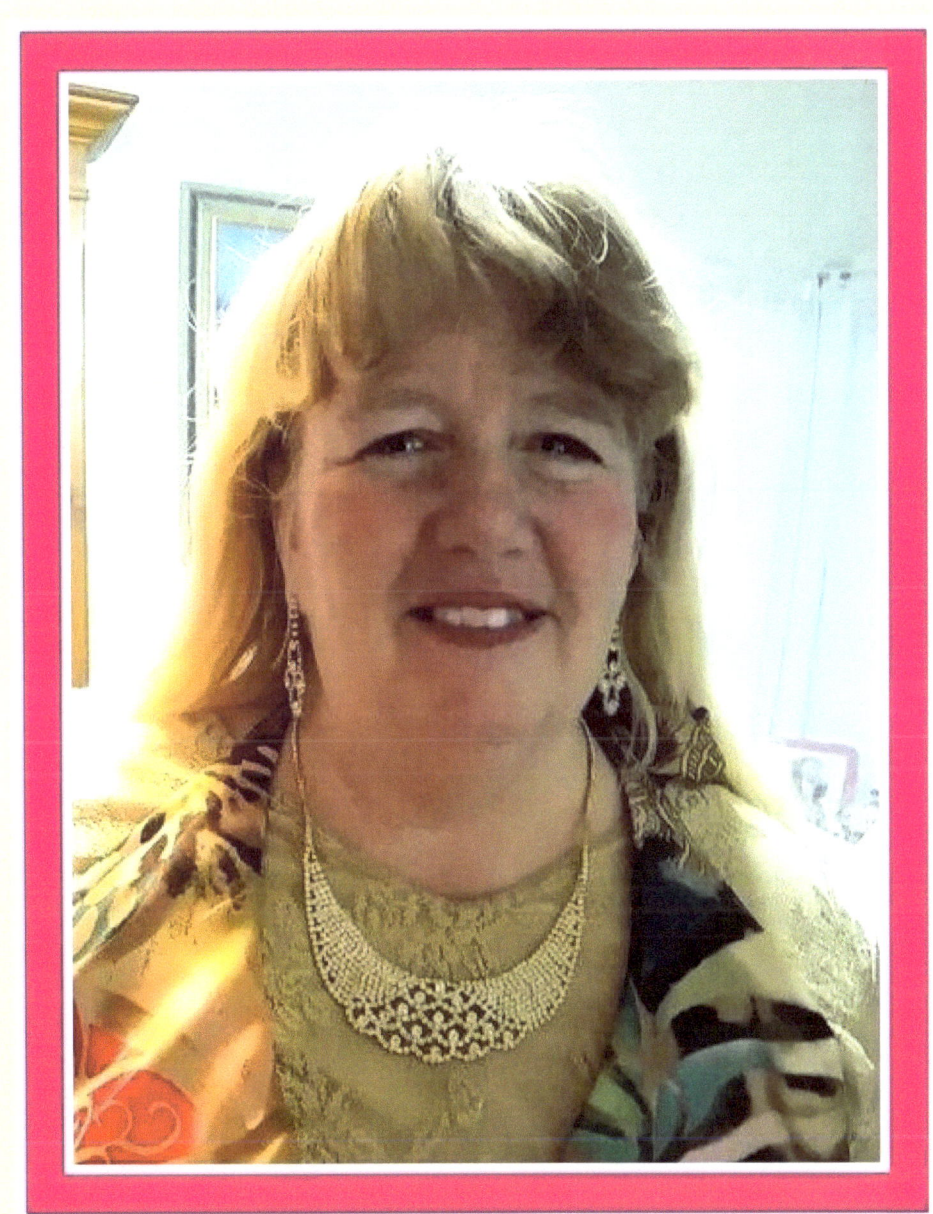

Author * Artist * Peggy Parrish